Birds *of* Prey
of the Northeast
FIELD GUIDE

by Stan Tekiela

Adventure Publications, Inc.
Cambridge, Minnesota

To all people who love the raptors as I do. May this book guide you through a lifetime of enjoying them all the more.

Acknowledgments

I would like to thank the following photographers, falconers, biologists and wonderful friends for their assistance in obtaining many of the amazing images in this book. I wish you all great success in each of your raptor endeavors.

Mark Alt, Grant Anderson, Rick and Nora Bowers, Amber Burnette, Peggy Callahan, Chase Delles, Deanne Endrizzi, Ron Green, Lee Greenly, Karla Kinstler, Andy Kramer, Mike Lentz, Jill Nezworski, Frank and Kate Nicolette, David and Adrienne Olson, Vic Peppe, Candy and Steve Ridlbauer, Pete Riola, Sam Riola, Sharon Stiteler, Frank Taylor, Brian K. Wheeler, Jim Zipp

Special thanks to Brian K. Wheeler, author, raptor expert, wildlife photographer and friend, for reviewing this field guide. Your extensive raptor knowledge is greatly appreciated.

Edited by Sandy Livoti

Cover and book design and nest illustrations by Jonathan Norberg

Quick-compare illustrations and raptor silhouettes by Dudley Edmondson except the Black Vulture by Julie Martinez.

Range maps by Anthony Hertzel

Cover photo: Peregrine Falcon by Stan Tekiela

See pages 168–169 for photo credits by photographer and page number.

Copyright 2011 by Stan Tekiela
Published by Adventure Publications, Inc.
820 Cleveland Street South
Cambridge, MN 55008
1-800-678-7006
www.adventurepublications.net
All rights reserved
Printed in China

ISBN: 978-1-59193-316-8

TABLE OF CONTENTS

BIRDS OF PREY OF THE NORTHEAST

Birds of prey are a diverse group of birds that have captured and held the attention of casual bird watchers and serious birders alike. Also known as raptors, these predatory birds include an amazing array of falcons, kites, hawks, eagles, vultures, owls and the Osprey. All varieties of raptors can be found during the day or throughout the night in nearly all habitats. Falcons are the fastest fliers, while kites are airborne acrobats, chasing insects high in the sky. Hawks, our most common raptor, are seen deep in the woods or hunting along forest edges, in open fields and over Northeastern meadows. Eagles and Ospreys are among the largest and most majestic birds of prey, visible near lakes and rivers. Most raptors are efficient predators, but vultures scavenge for their food without killing anything. Owls, both small and large, are flight masters of the dark.

Despite the wide diversity within the group, raptors physically have much in common. Many are large and powerful, with unsurpassed abilities to catch prey. In fact, the word "raptor" comes from the Latin term *rapere* and means "to seize or grab." Exceptionally strong feet, and toes tipped with dagger-like long nails are perfect for catching and killing small animals. A large curved bill allows raptors to tear flesh and crush bone. Raptors usually have relatively large eyes and better vision than people. Eagles, for example, can see much greater distances, and owls can see better in low-light environments. Most birds of prey have keen hearing—twice that of people. Many predatory birds are also masters of the sky, and people are fascinated by their flight. Propelled up by a single flap, they glide on outstretched wings to dizzying heights, or fly in almost total darkness. These extraordinary physical abilities set raptors apart from all other species of birds. It's no wonder we are thrilled by the sight of these magnificent creatures.

To help you enjoy these birds, *Birds of Prey of the Northeast Field Guide* has been designed as a handy pocket guide for quickly and easily identifying all 30 raptor species seen in the Northeast, including Connecticut, Delaware, Maine, Maryland, Massachusetts, New Hampshire, New Jersey, New York, Pennsylvania, Rhode Island and Vermont—a total of 11 states. Some species included this full-color photographic guide are more common than others. Only a few are considered rare.

TIPS FOR IDENTIFYING BIRDS OF PREY

Identifying raptors isn't as difficult as it may seem. Follow a few basic strategies, and you'll increase your chances of successfully identifying most birds of prey you see!

One of the first and easiest things to do when you see a new bird of prey is to note its overall shape. You won't always get a good look at a raptor, but noting the shape of its head, wings, tail or body may be all you need to identify it. Silhouettes of each raptor are provided on the description pages to help you confirm your identification. On quick-compare pages, photographs, illustrations and silhouettes will help you to identify a raptor whether it is in flight or perching.

Perching

Identifying a raptor that is perched on a tree branch, power pole or other object may be easier than trying to identify one that is flying. Unlike birds in flight, which often fly out of view quickly, perching birds allow you more time to observe them. In general, birds of prey will usually perch upright on branches or poles. This is unlike crows, ravens and other large birds or even smaller songbirds, which lean out over their feet and approach a more horizontal position. All of this changes, however, in strong winds, when nearly all raptors lean hard into the wind and sit nearly horizontal.

A perched falcon has a flat-topped, compact head, long tail and appears wider in the middle. Falcons often have bold, dark facial marks that appear like a mustache, called a malar, which help identify them while they perch. These birds tend to lean farther out over their feet (more like a songbird) than other birds of prey. Watch for some falcon species to pump their tails up and down directly after landing.

Kites perch upright with their long wings and tail projecting well beyond what you'd expect to see in a perching hawk. The round heads and long necks of kites will be obvious when they perch. Because these birds hunt while in flight, you will be more likely to see them flying to and from perches, chasing flying insects, rather than perched in a tree.

Buteo hawks are easy to identify when perched because of their relatively small heads, large broad bodies and short tails. They are frequently seen out in the open, along roads or in fields and prairies, making them easy to spot.

Smaller accipiters will rarely perch out in the open. Instead, these woodland hawks sit on tree branches for short periods, then fly off to other temporary perches in search of prey. They have smaller heads, narrower bodies, longer tails and less defined shoulders than buteos.

Harriers usually perch on the ground and occasionally on low posts. They have small heads, slender bodies and long narrow tails. Look for unusual owl-like facial disks to help identify this hawk when it is stationary.

Eagles are enormous birds of prey that perch bolt upright, often lowering their bodies over their legs and feet. They tend to look like the trunk of a tree when perching because they are so wide-bodied and dark. Just their size alone should be enough to identify them in a tree.

Ospreys appear eagle-like when perching, but they are smaller than eagles, with smaller heads and less impressive bills. Their long wings project well beyond their tails when perching. To differentiate an Osprey from an adult Bald Eagle, look for its white chest and belly.

Black Vultures and Turkey Vultures aren't often seen perching. When they do perch, they usually hold their wings outstretched to sun themselves, dry out their feathers after a rainstorm or warm up first thing in the morning after a cool night. While this behavior makes them easy to identify when stationary, you are more likely to see these birds flying. Look for their naked heads and dark bodies to help identify them.

Owls seen during the day usually will be perching, which often allows you to get a good look. These birds are easy to identify because they sit upright on branches, often with legs hidden in their belly feathers. They also have large round heads with large eyes positioned in front of their heads, thick compact bodies and short tails. Some owls have tufts of feathers on their heads, which appear like horns.

WHAT MAKES A BIRD OF PREY?

All predatory birds share some similar characteristics. Many have relatively large, sharp hooked bills to dispatch prey with a deep bite to the back of the neck at the base of the skull, which severs the spinal cord. Others squeeze prey to death or eat it alive. After a kill, raptors use their beaks to cut and tear flesh and crush bones.

With the exception of vultures, predatory birds have powerful feet, long toes and exceptionally sharp, long nails, called talons. Feet and toes are used to grasp and hold prey. Some birds can actually kill just with the feet. Eagles can do this, some exerting up to 500 pounds (225 kg) of pressure per square inch. Because feet are usually used to capture and hold prey, the importance of a raptor's foot cannot be overstated.

Powerful eyesight is probably the single most important feature of most birds of prey. Nearly all raptors hunt by using their eyes. Any damage to the eyes usually results in the demise of the bird. Eyes of raptors are large in proportion to their heads and fixed in their sockets. Larger eyes increase the vision power, but force a raptor to turn its head to look around. Owls, which have eyes positioned in the front of their faces, can see up to 100 times better than people in a low-light situation. Hawks, eagles and other raptors, which have eyes positioned more on the sides of their heads, can see at least 10 times better than people in daylight conditions. All raptors have two sets of eyelids. The outer eyelid is similar to a human eyelid and functions in nearly the same way in most birds. A thin, usually semitranslucent inner eyelid, called the nictitating membrane, cleans and moistens the cornea.

Besides keen eyesight, some raptors have outstanding hearing. Owls are known for hunting by sound. Their ears are hidden under feathers on the face, near the eyes. Great Horned Owls can hear a mouse under as much as a foot of snow. It is said that if an owl can see you, it can probably also hear your heart beat.

Most predatory birds are not brightly colored. Nearly all raptors are light to dark brown, black and white, grayish blue or some combination of earth tones. These colors help them to blend in with their environments.

RAPTOR ANATOMY

Males look identical to females in most raptor species. However, in many species females tend to be slightly or noticeably larger. Throughout the text, the words "slightly" or "noticeably" are used to describe size differences between sexes. When females are only 1–2 inches (2.5–5 cm) larger, "slightly" larger is used. Females at least 3 inches (7.5 cm) larger are referred to as "noticeably" larger. It is thought that egg laying, incubation and protection of eggs or young while still in the nest are reasons for this size discrepancy, or that since the male does most of the hunting, his smaller, more agile size allows him to be a more efficient hunter. Either way, it is not completely clear why in many species females are larger than males.

Juvenile raptors frequently don't appear like their parents for the first couple of years. They don't need the plumage of adult birds (such as the white head and tail of the adult Bald Eagle) to impress a mate, so they often have less dramatic plumage. Many predatory birds live long lives and take several years to become mature and sexually active, at which time they obtain adult breeding plumage.

It's easier to identify birds of prey and communicate about them when you know the names of the different parts of a bird. For instance, it's more effective to use the word "scapular" to describe the region on the back near the shoulder of a Red-tailed Hawk than to try to describe it.

Labeled images on the next two pages point out basic parts of a raptor. Because one image cannot show all the parts necessary, there are several examples of common birds of prey with labels. Every attempt has been made to label all parts of a bird with the terminology used in the text; however, not all terminology shown on the anatomy pages is used elsewhere in this book.

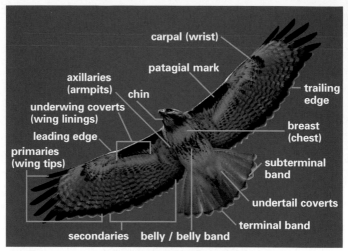

Underside (Ventral)

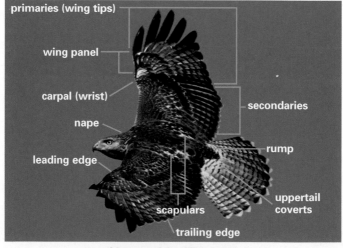

Upperside (Dorsal)

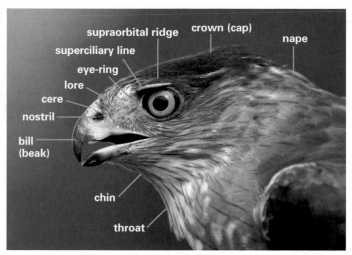

Facial Marking

Facial Marking

Unlike the predictable ebbing and flowing behavior of complete migrators or seasonal movement of partial migrators, **irruptive migrators** move unpredictably or only every third to fifth year or, in some cases, every tenth year. Irruptive migrations are triggered when times are very tough and food is scarce, or the population density of a species is too high. The Snowy Owl and Northern Goshawk are good examples of irruptive migrators. We can see them in some winters, while in other winters they are absent.

Migrating falcons, kites, hawks, eagles, Ospreys and vultures are daytime (diurnal) fliers that generally rest at night. They hunt early in the morning and begin migrating when soaring conditions are good, after the sun warms up the land. Migrators use a combination of landforms, rivers, and the rising and setting sun to guide them in the right direction. Slowly making their way south or north, they glide on rising columns of warm air (thermals), which hold them aloft. Wind also plays a big part. In autumn, migrators are helped by tailwinds from the north or northwest. These winds push birds along, enabling them to exert less energy than when fighting headwinds. Wind is equally important in the spring, with many birds returning when winds from the south are strong.

Non-migrators do not fly far from their home territory. Great Horned Owls, Eastern Screech-Owls and other non-migrators are usually sedentary birds that remain in the same area all year long. Ornithologists are now learning that some raptor varieties previously thought to be complete migrators are actually non-migrators. This is the case with Peregrine Falcons. For reasons that are not well understood, some races (subspecies) of this species migrate, while others do not.

HOW TO USE THIS GUIDE

This field guide was designed to be taken with you to help you identify raptors that you see flying or perching. The color photographs and accurate illustrations are ideal for anyone trying to learn more and identify birds of prey of the Northeast.

To help you quickly and easily identify birds of prey, this book is organized by species of birds. Falcons are first, followed by kites, hawks, eagles, the Osprey, vultures and owls. Individual sections are arranged by size beginning with the smaller birds. Sizes are in an average range that includes differences between similar-sized male and female birds, or separate male and female ranges when female birds are much larger than the males.

Special quick-compare pages, beginning on page 24, are useful for studying shapes, postures and colors of raptors. These pages are a great place to start the identification process and make overall comparisons among the birds. For a quick, easy reference, the photographs, illustrations and silhouettes are labeled with common names of the raptors, wingspans or body sizes and page numbers. Simply make comparisons with the bird you see. For detailed information and to confirm its identity, refer to the description pages.

Since many people first see a raptor when it's in flight, the first section of quick-compare pages consists of photographs of the 19 day raptors and 11 night raptors. These show what the birds look like during flight and are in order of wingspan size.

Because birds of prey often show a characteristic shape and noticeable field marks when they fly, the second quick-compare section presents illustrations of the 19 day raptors as they would appear in flight, by wingspan size. Since you are more likely to see perched owls, illustrations show the 11 night raptors as they would appear perching. The owls are organized by body size.

☀ DAY RAPTORS *Ordered by average body size*

FALCONS pg. 45 — 10"

American Kestrel

FALCONS pg. 49 — 11"

Merlin

HAWKS pg. 6? — 11"

Sharp-shinned Hawk

HAWKS pg. 81 — 17"

Red-shouldered Hawk

FALCONS pg. 53 — 17"

Peregrine Falcon

HAWKS pg. 85 — 18"

Northern Harrier

HAWKS pg. 97 — 22"

Red-tailed Hawk

FALCONS pg. 57 — 22"

Gyrfalcon

OSPREY pg. 109 — 23"

Osprey

KITES   pg. 61
13"

Mississippi Kite

HAWKS   pg. 73

Cooper's Hawk

HAWKS   pg. 77
17"

Broad-winged Hawk

KITES   pg. 65
20"

Swallow-tailed Kite

HAWKS   pg. 89
20"

Rough-legged Hawk

HAWKS   pg. 93
21"

Northern Goshawk

VULTURES   pg. 113
27"

Black Vulture

VULTURES   pg. 117
29"

Turkey Vulture

EAGLES   pg. 101
33"

Golden Eagle

☀ DAY RAPTORS *Ordered by average body size*

EAGLES   pg. 105

34"

Bald Eagle

🌙 NIGHT RAPTORS (OWLS) *Ordered by average body size*

OWLS   pg. 121

7"

Northern Saw-whet Owl

OWLS   pg. 125

9"

Eastern Screech-Owl

OWLS   pg. 129

10"

Boreal Owl

OWLS   pg. 145

17"

Barn Owl

OWLS   pg. 149

22"

Barred Owl

OWLS   pg. 153

23"

Great Horned Owl

Long-eared Owl

Northern Hawk Owl

Short-eared Owl

Snowy Owl

Great Gray Owl

Common Name

Scientific name

AR-ROUND
IIGRATION
SUMMER
WINTER
NCOMMON

Family: common family name (scientific family name)

Size: (L) average range of length from head to tail; may include (M) male and (F) female lengths; (WS) average range of wingspan

Weight: average range of weight; may include (M) male and (F) female weights

Male: complete description; some include color morphs or other plumages

Female: physical description compared with the male

Juvenile: full description, often compared with the adults; some include facts about maturation or size

Habitat: environment of the raptor (e.g., forests, prairies, agricultural fields, meadows, mountains, cliffs, backyards, parks, roadsides, wetlands, rivers, lakes, reservoirs, bogs)

Food: what the raptor eats most of the time (e.g., birds, small mammals, reptiles, amphibians, insects, fish, carrion)

Sounds: calls or other vocalizations made by the male or female; may also include juvenile calls or noises created in flight

Compare: Notes about other raptors that look similar and the pages on which they are found. May include extra information to help identify.

Flight: identifying features of the raptor as seen in flight; how the raptor flies; wing beats; types of flight

Migration: complete (regular, seasonal migration patterns), partial (seasonal movement, but destination varies), irruptive (unpredictable movement, depends on the food supply), non-migrator (year-round resident); may include more information

Nesting: kind of nest the raptor constructs and the location; who builds the nest and description of nesting materials; how many broods per year

Eggs/Incubation: number of eggs, color and marking; who does the most incubation and average incubation time; how the incubating parent obtains food

Fledging: average time the young remain in the nest after they hatch and before they leave the nest; who does the most "child-care" and feeding; feeding response of the young

Stan's Notes: Interesting gee-whiz natural history information. This can be something to look or listen for, or something to help positively identify the bird such as remarkable features, unique behaviors and other key characteristics.

male

male diving

female

male
juvenile

female

Flight: pointed swept-back wings; rapid, shallow wing beats alternate with short to long gliding; hovers nears roads before diving to catch prey; flicks tail up and down immediately after landing

Migration: complete migrator, to southern states, Mexico and Central America; others are partial to non-migrators, moving around during winter in search of food, sometimes from rural to urban areas; small percentage remain all winter when food is plentiful

Nesting: cavity, in a tree, cliff face or wooden nest box; does not build a nest within; 1 brood

Eggs/Incubation: 4–5 white eggs with brown markings; male and female incubate 29–31 days; male does the most hunting and feeds the female during incubation

Fledging: 30–31 days; female and male feed young; male does the majority of hunting and brings food to the female, who feeds the chicks; upon leaving the nest (fledging), the young continue to beg for food and are very vocal, chasing parents around after they capture prey; chicks learn to hunt by watching and copying the behavior of their parents and are hunting by the end of their first summer

Stan's Notes: The American Kestrel is an unusual raptor. Not only do the male and female have different markings (dichromatic), the female is larger than the male (dimorphic).

A falcon, sometimes called K-bird. Was once known as Sparrow Hawk due to its small size. Could be called Grasshopper Hawk because it consumes many grasshoppers. Has the ability to see ultraviolet light. This helps it find mice and other mammals by their urine, which glows bright yellow in ultraviolet light.

Has pointed swept-back wings, seen during flight. Hovers near roads before diving for prey. Perches nearly upright. To help identify this raptor from a distance, watch for it to pump its tail up and down after landing on a perch. While some individuals have been known to become habituated to people, others can be skittish and will fly away when approached.

Adapts quickly to a Wood Duck nest box that is mounted on poles about 7–10 feet (2.1–3 m) aboveground. After the breeding season, kestrels often gather together (gregarious), migrating and wintering in loosely formed groups. Can be antagonistic toward other raptors while in groups, chasing and harassing larger birds until they leave the area.

male

Merlin

Falco columbarius

SUMMER
WINTER

Family: Falcons (Falconidae)

Size: L 10–12" (25–30 cm); WS 18–24" (45–61 cm)

Weight: 5½–6½ oz. (156–184 g)

Male: Steel blue back with darker head and tail. Rusty wash to upper breast, sides, wing linings (underwing coverts), undertail coverts and leg feathers. Heavily streaked breast and underwings. Light line above each eye (superciliary). Weak vertical mustache markings (malar). Distinctive wide black subterminal tail band and 1-3 very narrow white tail bands.

Female: similar to male, slightly larger, brown head and back, very difficult to tell apart from the male, 1–3 very narrow buffy tail bands

Juvenile: similar to adult female

Habitat: forests, wooded backyards, rural to urban areas

Food: birds, insects, small mammals and reptiles

Sounds: can be very vocal in all seasons; female voice is lower and slower than that of the male; young are the most vocal, especially immediately after fledging, repeating a high-pitched "kee-kee-kee"

Compare: American Kestrel (pg. 45) is overall more rusty and has bold vertical mustache marks (malar). The Peregrine Falcon (pg. 53) has a white face and bold mustache marks. Merlin is the only raptor with multiple narrow tail bands.

adult

juvenile
dorsal

juvenile

female

Flight: narrow pointed wings and dark underwings; very fast and direct, purposeful flight; powerful, rapid wing beats interspersed with short to long gliding; flicks tail up and down immediately after landing

Migration: complete migrator, to the East Coast, Gulf Coast states, Central and South America

Nesting: platform, or cavity on a cliff; takes an old crow or hawk nest and relines it with twigs and some feathers; 1 brood

Eggs/Incubation: 4–7 white eggs with rust brown markings; male and female incubate 28–32 days; male does the most hunting and feeds the female during incubation

Fledging: 30–35 days; female and male feed young; male does the majority of hunting and brings food to the female, who feeds the chicks; upon leaving the nest (fledging), the young still beg for food and are very vocal, chasing parents around after they capture prey; chicks learn to hunt by copying their parents and are hunting by the end of their first summer

Stan's Notes: There are three races of Merlin—Taiga, Prairie (not shown) and Pacific (not shown). Each is slightly different from the other in markings and range of color. Only the Taiga is found in the Northeast.

Formerly called Pigeon Hawk. Also known as Blue-backed Jack due to the blue color of the adult male's back. Narrow pointed wings, dark underwings and the lack of bold facial markings help to identify this woodland hunter.

Feeds on birds more than insects or small animals. Catches most of its prey in flight, giving a burst of speed close to the ground rather than diving or hovering like the other falcons.

In urban areas, nests in tall conifers and seems to prefer House Finches. Appears to move into urban areas in winter, but nests in the northern coniferous forests of Canada. Males return to the same breeding territory before the females. The male hunts and provides food for the female during courtship to show he would be a good provider while she incubates. Monogamous, with long-term pair bonding. Nests alone. Defends territory against other birds of prey, including other Merlins. Sometimes young males help other adult males defend territory.

Peregrine Falcon

Falco peregrinus

YEAR-ROUND
MIGRATION
SUMMER

Family: Falcons (Falconidae)

Size: M 14–16" (36–40 cm); WS 3–3¼' (.9–1 m)
F 16–20" (40–50 cm); WS 3¼–3¾' (1–1.14 m)

Weight: M 1–1¼ lb. (.5–.6 kg); F 1¼–1½ lb. (.6–.7 kg)

Male: A wide-bodied raptor. Dark, nearly black head marking resembling a hood. Steel blue back and tail. Pale white-to-tan breast and underwings. Small black horizontal bars on belly, legs, underwings and undertail. Black mustache markings (malar). Yellow base of bill (cere), eye-rings, legs and feet. Some individuals have a wash of salmon on the breast.

Female: similar to male, noticeably larger

Juvenile: mostly brown with heavy vertical streaks on the breast and belly, overall darker than adults

Habitat: along rivers, lakes, forests, cliffs, bluffs, city parks, along highways and other roadways, rural to urban areas

Food: birds (Rock Pigeons in many cities, shorebirds and waterfowl in rural areas)

Sounds: usually repeats a loud, harsh alarm call near the nest; young give a similar call to beg for food

Compare: The Gyrfalcon (pg. 57) is larger and lacks the black hood. The American Kestrel (pg. 45) is much smaller, brightly colored and lacks a blackish hood. Peregrine Falcon is usually identified by its dark head marking, mustache marks and clear upper breast.

Flight: long pointed wings; deep, smooth, powerful wing beats interspersed with short gliding; soars with wings flat, often riding thermals

Migration: complete migrator, to southern states, Mexico, Central and South America; a few non-migrators stay in parts of the Northeast all year

Nesting: ground (scrape), on a cliff edge; nest is just a shallow depression scraped in the dirt; will also use an artificial (man-made) wooden platform with a dirt and rock bottom, installed on a tall building; not lined with nesting material; 1 brood

Eggs/Incubation: 3–4 white eggs, occasionally with brown markings; female and male incubate 29–32 days; male does the most hunting and feeds the female during incubation

Fledging: 35–42 days; female feeds the young; male does the majority of hunting and brings food to the female, who feeds the chicks; upon leaving the nest (fledging), the young still beg for food and are very vocal; chicks learn to hunt by watching and copying the behavior of their parents and are hunting by the end of their first summer

Stan's Notes: A hunter of many species of birds, especially pigeons and waterfowl. All birds scatter at the approach of a Peregrine Falcon.

Became locally extinct in many regions (extirpated) due to DDT poisoning during the 1930–60s. Was reintroduced by a captive breeding program and released into cities starting in the 1980s. It has since made a great comeback and is doing well. In some areas it may even be more common than it was historically.

Females are noticeably larger than the males. When they hunt together, the female will take the lead and capture larger prey. Hunts by diving (stooping) on pigeons at speeds up to 175 mph (282 km/h) or more, knocking the prey from sky to ground.

Prefers nesting on ledges for a good view of its territory, which is why it has taken so well to high buildings, bridges and tall smokestacks. To provide more nesting habitat, platforms with rocks and gravel have been installed near building ledges.

Monogamous and a solitary nester. During courtship, performs aerial displays and male brings food to the female.

gray morph

Gyrfalcon
Falco rusticolus

FALCONS

WINTER

Family: Falcons (Falconidae)

Size: M 19–22" (48–56 cm); WS 3½–4' (1.1–1.2 m)
F 22–25" (56–64 cm); WS 4–4¼' (1.2–1.3 m)

Weight: M 2–2½ lb. (.9–1.1 kg); F 2½–3 lb. (1.1–1.4 kg)

Male: Largest falcon worldwide, appearing in a variety of colors from gray to dark brown to nearly all white. Yellow base of bill (cere), eye-rings and legs. When perching, the wing tips do not reach the end of tail. **Gray morph** has a gunmetal gray head, back and wings, with many dark markings on a light breast and belly. **Dark morph** is dark brown to nearly black, with a dark head marking that looks like a hood. **White morph** has a white head, breast and belly, with many dark bars on the back and wings.

Female: similar to male, noticeably larger

Juvenile: overall light brown with streaking throughout, underwings are two-toned with a paler trailing edge, tail is wider and longer than the adult tail, has a bluish cere, eye-rings and legs

Habitat: prairies, rock outcrops, tundra

Food: birds (especially ptarmigans and pigeons), small mammals

Sounds: repeats a deep, harsh "kaik-kaik-kaik" alarm call; juvenile call sounds similar

Compare: Peregrine Falcon (pg. 53) is smaller, with a nearly black head marking that looks like a hood, and narrower, more pointed wings.

adult dark

adult white

juvenile gray

chicks

gray morph

Flight: long broad wings with rounded tips; stiff, shallow wing beats alternate with short gliding; flies low when hunting; soars on thermals

Migration: partial migrator in parts of the upper Northeast, appearing only in winter when a few individuals leave their normal range; moves around during winter in search of food

Nesting: no nest, scrape in dirt on the edge of a cliff; 1 brood

Eggs/Incubation: 3–5 white eggs with brown markings; female and male incubate 34–36 days; male does the most hunting and feeds the female during incubation

Fledging: 49–56 days; male and female feed young; male does the majority of hunting and brings food to the female, who feeds the chicks; upon leaving the nest (fledging), the young continue to beg for food and are very vocal; chicks learn to hunt by watching and copying the behavior of their parents and are hunting by the end of their first summer

Stan's Notes: The largest and most powerful of falcons, but not common anywhere in the Northeast. A falconry bird that historically was reserved for kings for sport hunting. Gray is the most common color morph; white is the least common.

Usually a non-migrator. Some individuals, often females, move south in late autumn, spending the winter in upper parts of the Northeast. Once it takes up winter residency, it often remains all winter, leaving late in the season. Seen infrequently.

Breeds on rock outcrops in the Arctic tundra of Canada and Alaska. Monogamous and a solitary nester, with only one pair around for many miles.

May skip nesting entirely when prey is scarce. Hunts by flying low, capturing prey by surprise. In its normal range it relies on the ptarmigan, a grouse-like bird, as its main food source. The number of Gyrfalcons increases and decreases with the abundance of ptarmigans. Usually feeds on pigeons when out of its normal range.

Mississippi Kite

Ictinia mississippiensis

Family: Hawks, Eagles and Kites (Accipitridae)

Size: L 12–15" (30–38 cm); WS 29–33" (74–84 cm)

Weight: 9–11 oz. (255–312 g)

Male: Overall gray bird with a paler, nearly white head and nearly black tail and tips of wings. Dark eye patch surrounding red eyes. Yellow legs and feet. Short, hooked gray bill. Wings have white secondaries, seen in flight from above, and rusty primaries, seen from above and below.

Female: same as male, slightly larger, head not as white

Juvenile: brown breast with white horizontal streaks, alternate dark and light bands on the tail, rusty wing linings (underwing coverts) seen in flight, dark wing tips (primaries) and secondaries

Habitat: fields with scattered tall trees, backyards, parks, near rivers or streams, suburban to urban areas

Food: butterflies, cicadas, other large insects, lizards, small snakes

Sounds: very high-pitched, weak whistle call, descending in pitch when trespassers get near the nest; can be very vocal during breeding season

Compare: Slightly larger than Sharp-shinned Hawk (pg. 69) and smaller than the Cooper's Hawk (pg. 73). The Kite's overall gray appearance with the light-colored head and long pointed wings makes it easy to identify. Look for the dark tail and light head to help identify it during flight.

Flight: long pointed wings; wide variety of flight patterns since it hunts for insects in midair; glides with wings fully out-stretched and flat when eating in flight; buoyant flight, soaring with wings flat; wings often swept back when diving

Migration: complete migrator, to South America

Nesting: platform, often in a deciduous tree, near the top; female and male build a small, shallow, flimsy nest; 1 brood

Eggs/Incubation: 1–2 white eggs; female and male incubate 29–32 days; each parent hunts for its own food, but both feed the young

Fledging: 32–34 days; female and male feed the young still in the nest; male does the majority of the hunting and feeding of young after they fledge; young sit on a branch and give a high-pitched whistle to beg for food; parents bring food and pass it quickly to the young before taking off to hunt again; chicks learn to hunt by watching and copying the behavior of parents and are hunting by the end of their first summer

Stan's Notes: A bird of prey that feeds mostly on large insects, taking advantage of large hatches of cicadas and butterflies. Several kites can be seen following livestock, feeding on insects kicked up by the animals. Hunts by soaring or hovering, catching prey in flight or diving down to snatch an insect from tree branches and leaves. Can dive very fast, pulling up suddenly to land softly and smoothly on a branch.

Requires open areas with scattered tall trees for nesting. Will sometimes nest in small colonies of up to 20 pairs, with nests evenly spaced among trees. Leisurely paced mating and nesting; some wait to nest until late summer. Mated pairs aggressively defend nest sites. Often doesn't nest until 2 years of age.

Courting males bring food to females. Non-breeding birds (sub-adults) often form groups within colonies. Sometimes they help construct nests and feed the new young.

Individuals often stray out of their traditional ranges and appear in northern states, as well as up the East Coast. Was once found farther east and in much higher populations. Decline has been due to the destruction of lowland forests along river bottoms, pesticide use, indiscriminate shooting and poisoning.

Swallow-tailed Kite

Elanoides forficatus

COMMON

Family: Hawks, Eagles and Kites (Accipitridae)

Size: L 18–23" (45–58 cm); WS 4–4½' (1.2–1.3 m)

Weight: 14–16 oz. (397–454 g)

Male: White head, breast and belly. Black back, wings and tail. Long, narrow pointed wings. White underwing coverts and black trailing edge, seen during flight. Long, deeply forked tail. Back and wings change color with light conditions, appearing metallic greenish blue.

Female: same as male

Juvenile: similar to adults, with a shorter tail and buffy brown wash to the head and chest that lasts only a few weeks

Habitat: open woods, near river bottoms, fields with scattered tall trees, backyards, parks, near streams, suburban to urban areas

Food: large insects such as bees, butterflies, dragonflies, beetles and cicadas; also eats lizards, small snakes, frogs, small mammals

Sounds: very high-pitched, weak whistle call, descending in pitch when intruders are near the nest; can be very vocal during breeding season

Compare: Osprey (pg. 109) is similar in size and shares the black and white pattern, but lacks a long forked tail. Mississippi Kite (pg. 61) is much smaller than Swallow-tailed and is gray with a black tail that does not fork. No other bird of prey in the Northeast has a forked tail as deep as the Swallow-tailed Kite. Rare in the Northeast.

juvenile

adult

juvenile

Flight: long, narrow pointed wings and forked tail; many flight patterns because it hunts insects in midair; glides with wings fully outstretched and flat when eating in flight; buoyant, agile flight, soaring with wings flat and the forked tail opening and closing like scissors; wings often swept back when diving; rarely hovers, but soars on thermals extensively; gathers in flocks for winter migration

Migration: complete migrator, to the tropics of Central and South America

Nesting: platform, often in a deciduous tree, near the top; female and male build a small, shallow, flimsy nest; 1 brood

Eggs/Incubation: 2–4 white eggs with dark markings; female and male incubate 26–28 days; each parent hunts for its own food; both parents feed the young

Fledging: 36–42 days; female and male feed the young still in the nest; male does the majority of the hunting and feeding of young after they fledge; young sit on a branch and give a high-pitched whistle to beg for food; parents bring food and pass it quickly to the young before taking off to hunt again; chicks learn to hunt by watching and copying the behavior of parents and are hunting by the end of their first summer

Stan's Notes: Rarely seen, ranging into parts of the Northeast in some years. Found mostly in Florida, Georgia and South Carolina. Nested in the Northeast during the 1800s, but by the early 1900s the breeding range crashed due to changing habitats. It is thought that just 800–1,500 pairs nest in the United States in any given year, producing a total of about 4,000–4,500 individuals at the end of the breeding season. Semisocial, with several individuals sharing the same territory.

Stunning in flight. Easily identified by its contrasting colors and forked tail. Feeds during flight. Also drinks on the wing, skimming across the water like a swallow. Soars with wings flat, riding thermals high into the air. Rarely hovers like other raptors. An agile flier, collecting sticks for its nest much like the Osprey (pg. 109), breaking off sticks from dead trees with its feet during flight. One study estimated that over 200 items, such as twigs and pine needle sprigs, all carried singly, were used to build a nest.

Majority of the diet includes bees, butterflies, dragonflies and beetles, which are caught and eaten in flight. Will also snatch lizards and large insects, such as cicadas, from leaves of trees.

Sharp-shinned Hawk

Accipiter striatus

Family: Hawks, Eagles and Kites (Accipitridae)

YEAR-ROUND
SUMMER
WINTER

Size: M 9–11" (23–28 cm); WS 20–22" (50–56 cm)
F 11–13" (28–33 cm); WS 23–26" (58–66 cm)

Weight: 3½–5 oz. (99–142 g)

Male: A small woodland hawk with a tiny round head. Bluish gray back and head. Rusty red horizontal barring on a white chest. Long squared-off tail. Several dark tail bands, widest band at the end. Large orange-to-red eyes. Short yellow legs and long thin toes. In flight, the head barely projects past the bend of wings (wrists), which are often thrust forward.

Female: same as male, noticeably larger, up to one-third more than the male, with a gray back

Juvenile: same size as adults, with a brown back, heavy vertical streaking on the chest, bright yellow-to-orange eyes

Habitat: wooded backyards, woodlands, forests, parks

Food: small birds, small animals, reptiles, amphibians

Sounds: screams a high-pitched, whistle-like repetitive call when interlopers get close to the nest; can be very vocal during breeding season

Compare: Cooper's Hawk (pg. 73) is larger, has a larger head, smaller eyes, longer legs, slightly longer neck and a rounded tip of tail. During flight, the head of the Sharp-shinned does not protrude as far as the Cooper's. Red-shouldered Hawk (pg. 81) has a reddish head and belly and lacks a gray back. Look for the squared tip of tail to help identify the Sharp-shinned Hawk.

Flight: short rounded wings and long narrow tail; head does not extend beyond the bend in wrist; fast, shallow wing beats interspersed with short gliding; soars in groups during migration on rising columns of warm air

Migration: complete migrator in the northern portion of the Northeast; non-migrator throughout much of the region; found along the coast during winter

Nesting: platform, in a mature tree in thick deciduous woods, usually in the first fork or crotch near the main trunk, made of sticks, twigs and branches with green leaves; female builds a new nest or repairs an old one with new material; 1 brood

Eggs/Incubation: 4–5 white eggs with brown markings; female incubates 32–35 days; male does the most hunting and feeds the nesting female before and after the young hatch

Fledging: 24–27 days; female feeds the young; male does the majority of hunting and brings food to the female, who feeds the chicks; upon leaving the nest (fledging), the young still beg for food; chicks learn to hunt by watching and copying the behavior of the parents and are hunting by the end of their first summer; young migrate on their own, separate from the adults

Stan's Notes: This is a common small hawk that often can be seen swooping down on birds at your feeders. Its short rounded wings and long tail allow it to navigate through thick stands of trees during fast pursuit of prey. Common name comes from the sharp keel on the leading edge of its "shin," although it is actually below rather than above the bird's ankle on the tarsus bone of the foot. The tarsus in most birds is round.

The smallest of the American accipiters. Its head is so small that its eyes appear large, even though they are about the same size as those of the Cooper's Hawk (pg. 73). A true bird hunter. Of all accipiters, it takes more birds than other types of prey.

Often seen more during fall migration, moving south in large numbers from Canada. Each fall the juveniles migrate weeks before the adults. Although frequently seen in groups during migration, Sharp-shins migrate alone during the day, hunting for food early in the morning before the thermals start building in late morning.

Courtship is usually near the nest site. Pairs fly in circles, call to one another and land beside each other on a branch.

Cooper's Hawk

Accipiter cooperii

YEAR-ROUND
SUMMER

Family: Hawks, Eagles and Kites (Accipitridae)

Size: M 14–16" (36–40 cm); WS 28–30" (71–76 cm)
F 16–19" (40–48 cm); WS 31–34" (79–86 cm)

Weight: 12–16 oz. (340–454 g)

Male: Medium hawk with a blue-gray head, neck, back and upperwings. Rusty red horizontal barring on a white breast. Large squared head. Dark crown. Orange-to-red eyes. Long tail, rounded tip (terminal) with a few dark bands and wide light band. In flight, head projects well past the wrists, which are usually not thrust forward. Long yellow legs and feet.

Female: similar to male, noticeably larger, up to one-third more than the male, with a gray back

Juvenile: brown head and back, vertical brown streaks on a white breast, pale yellow eyes

Habitat: woodlands, forests, wooded backyards, parks

Food: small birds, mammals, reptiles, amphibians

Sounds: screams a repetitive nasal "cack-cack-cack-cack" call when trespassers are near the nest; can be very vocal during breeding season

Compare: Larger than the Sharp-shinned Hawk (pg. 69), with a larger head, darker cap, longer legs and rounded tail, not a squared tail. Unlike Sharp-shinned, Cooper's wings are perpendicular to the body, usually not thrust forward in flight. Eyes look smaller than those of Sharp-shinned, but only because the Cooper's head is so much larger. The juvenile Cooper's has pale yellow eyes, not bright yellow eyes like juvenile Sharp-shinned.

Broad-winged Hawk

Buteo platypterus

SUMMER

Family: Hawks, Eagles and Kites (Accipitridae)

Size: L 14–19" (36–48 cm); WS 30–36" (76–91 cm)

Weight: 10–17 oz. (284–482 g)

Male: Brown-to-tan head, back and upperwings. Thick, rusty horizontal bars or V-shaped markings on the breast. Most have a solid rusty brown breast, forming a bib. Eyes brown to pale orange. Short wide wings. White underwings, black "finger-tips" (primaries) and a dark trailing edge. Rusty brown axillaries. Wide dark subterminal tail band with a white edge. This species has a dark morph, but it is very uncommon; overall dark brown with 2 wide black tail bands and a white band in between.

Female: same as male, slightly larger

Juvenile: vertical brown streaks on the breast and belly, narrow dusky gray band on the trailing edge of wings, numerous narrow gray tail bands

Habitat: forests, woodlands, wooded backyards, parks

Food: snakes, frogs, toads, small birds, small mammals, large insects

Sounds: repeats a high-pitched, whistle-like screaming call when intruders are close to the nest

Compare: Similar size as Red-shouldered Hawk (pg. 81), but lacks the rufous shoulders and white spots on wings and back. Cooper's Hawk (pg. 73) has a gray back, rusty chest and belly and longer, narrower tail. Look for the rusty brown bib on the breast to help identify the Broad-winged Hawk.

adult

adult dorsal

juvenile

juvenile

adult dark

Flight: large barrel-shaped body, relatively short tail and broad wings, wider at the center with rounded wing tips and short "fingertips" (primaries); shallow, rapid wing beats interspersed with short to long gliding; during migration, soars in groups (kettles) on rising columns of warm air

Migration: complete migrator, to the southern tip of Florida, southern Mexico, Central and South America

Nesting: platform, in a mature tree in dense deciduous woods, usually in the first fork or crotch, constructed with sticks, twigs and branches with green leaves still attached; female and male construct a new nest each year or repair an old nest, bringing in new nesting material; 1 brood

Eggs/Incubation: 2–3 off-white eggs with brown markings; female incubates 28–32 days; male does the most hunting and feeds the nesting female before and after the young hatch

Fledging: 34–40 days; female and male feed young; male does the most hunting and brings food to the female, who feeds the chicks; upon leaving the nest (fledging), young beg for food, chasing their parents after they capture prey; chicks watch the parents hunt and are hunting by the end of their first summer

Stan's Notes: A forest buteo hawk, common in the Northeast. Often heard before seen when disturbed around the nest. Can be aggressive near the nest, dive-bombing human trespassers. Spends most of its time perching, hunting for small birds, snakes and frogs in dense woodlands. Its short rounded wings help it maneuver safely in thick forests. Sky-dance courtship flights include steep closed-wing dives, terminating with a sharp upward flight, rolling over and flying upside down. Often very vocal during courtship.

A highly migratory hawk and the most abundant migrating hawk species at hawk watch locations every fall. Seen in large clusters during fall and spring migration, swirling in tight groups known as kettles. Very punctual during migration, with juvenile birds moving through the upper Northeast in large groups in early September, followed by adults mid-month. By the second week of October most have moved through.

Also called Broadwing or Broadie, and Aguililla Alas Anchas or Aguililla Aluda in Spanish. The dark morph of this species is extremely uncommon in the Northeast.

Red-shouldered Hawk

Buteo lineatus

R-ROUND
UMMER

Family: Hawks, Eagles and Kites (Accipitridae)

Size: L 15–19" (38–48 cm); WS 3–3½' (.9–1.1 m)

Weight: 10–17 oz. (284–482 g)

Male: A medium-sized hawk with a cinnamon (rufous) head, shoulders, breast and belly. Upperwings and back are dark brown to nearly black, with white spots covering upperwings. Long rounded tail has thin, light tail bands alternating with wide black bands. Rufous wing linings (underwing coverts), obvious during flight.

Female: same as male, slightly larger

Juvenile: similar to adults, lacks the rusty red color, has a white breast with dark vertical streaking and several narrow bands on the tail

Habitat: wooded backyards, forests, woodlands, parks, roadsides

Food: reptiles, amphibians, large insects, small birds

Sounds: very vocal; repeats a distinctive, high-pitched clear whistle or screaming call when interlopers get near the nest and during breeding season

Compare: The Cooper's Hawk (pg. 73) also has a rufous breast and belly, but is overall thinner and has a much longer tail. Broad-winged Hawk (pg. 77) lacks the rusty red wing linings. Red-tailed Hawk (pg. 97) is larger and has a white breast.

adult

juvenile

juvenile

mother and chicks

Flight: long broad wings, wider at the center, with rounded wing tips, short "fingertips" (primaries) and a white crescent-shaped pattern across the base of the wing tips; tail relatively short and wide; flaps with fast, stiff wing beats alternating with a gliding pattern; soars in groups during migration on rising columns of warm air

Migration: complete to non-migrator, moving out of the upper half of the Northeast, with many remaining in the southern part of the region all year; moves around in winter to find food

Nesting: platform, in a mature tree in dense deciduous woods, usually in the first fork or crotch near the main trunk, made with sticks, twigs and branches that have green leaves attached; female and male repair an old nest or build a new nest each year; 1 brood

Eggs/Incubation: 2–4 white eggs with dark markings; female and male incubate 27–29 days; male does the most hunting and feeds the nesting female before and after the young hatch

Fledging: 39–45 days; female feeds the young; male does the majority of hunting and brings food to the female, who feeds the chicks; upon leaving the nest (fledging), the young still beg for food; chicks learn to hunt by copying the parents' behavior and are hunting by the end of their first summer

Stan's Notes: A common woodland hawk in the Northeast. Seen in wooded backyards and parks, tolerating the presence of people well. Likes to hunt forest edges, spotting frogs, snakes, insects, an occasional bird and other prey while perching.

Adults return to the same nest and territory for many years; the young also return. Starts nest building in February, with young leaving the nest by June. Matures sexually at 2–3 years of age.

Two groups of hawks—buteos and accipiters. Buteos, such as Red-tailed Hawks (pg. 97), are open country hawks. Accipiters, such as Sharp-shinned and Cooper's Hawks (pp. 69 and 73, respectively), are woodland hawks. The Red-shouldered Hawk is unique because it is a forest buteo more closely related to Red-tailed Hawk (which hunts in open country) than to the forest-dwelling Sharp-shinned and Cooper's Hawks.

Three races (subspecies) are recognized in North America—Eastern, Florida (not shown) and California (not shown). One of the few hawk species besides the Red-tailed with different color variations (subspecies) in different parts of the country.

male

Northern Harrier
Circus cyaneus

YEAR-ROUND
SUMMER
WINTER

Family: Hawks, Eagles and Kites (Accipitridae)

Size: M 16–18" (40–45 cm); WS 3¼–3½' (1–1.1 m)
F 18–20" (45–50 cm); WS 3½–4' (1.1–1.2 m)

Weight: 12–15 oz. (340–425 g)

Male: Light gray head and silver gray back and upper-wings. White underwings, belly and large rump patch. Faint streaking on chest. Faint tail bands. Black wing tips and black trailing edge of wings. Owl-like facial disks. Yellow eyes and dark bill.

Female: noticeably larger than the male, head and back are dark to rusty brown, vertical brown streaks on chest and belly, large white rump patch, thin black bands on tail, owl-like facial disks, yellow eyes, small dark bill

Juvenile: similar to the adult female, orange breast without vertical streaks, eyes are dark brown to tan

Habitat: open fields, marshes, wetlands, meadows, parks

Food: small mammals, snakes, insects, small birds

Sounds: usually silent; repeats a sharp call if trespassers come near the nest; gives a short high-pitched whistle like that of Broad-winged Hawk (pg. 77)

Compare: Slimmer and has a longer tail than Red-tailed Hawk (pg. 97). Turkey Vulture (pg. 117) shares a similar tilting flight pattern, but is much larger, darker and lacks the white rump patch. Short-eared Owl (pg. 141) shares the facial disks and has a similar characteristic low flight pattern, but the Harrier has a longer tail and white rump patch. Look for the black tail bands, white rump patch and characteristic flight to help identify.

adult light

juvenile light

adult dark

juvenile light dorsal

juvenile dark

juvenile light

juvenile dark

dark morph

Flight: relatively long wings and long tail; deep, full wing beats interspersed with short gliding; faces into strong wind and hovers, looking for prey; may pump its wings hard to stall flight for a short time when the wind is mild

Migration: complete migrator, to the Northeast and upper half of the United States during winter; moves around in groups of up to 10–25 individuals, remaining together all winter

Nesting: platform, on top of a small tree, on the edge of a cliff, constructed with sticks, twigs and branches, lined with grasses and feathers; female and male build a new nest each year or repair an old nest, adding new nesting material; 1 brood

Eggs/Incubation: 2–6 white eggs; female incubates 28–31 days; male does the most hunting and feeds the nesting female before and after the young hatch

Fledging: 39–43 days; female feeds the young; male does the majority of hunting and brings food to the female, who feeds the chicks; when the young leave the nest (fledge), they still continue to beg for food; chicks learn to hunt by watching and copying the behavior of their parents and are hunting by the end of their first summer

Stan's Notes: Named for the feathers on its legs. This hawk appears in two color morphs, light and dark. The light morph is more common, but both are seen together.

Nests in Alaska, Canada's Northwest Territories and east to Newfoundland, moving into the Northeast in winter. More numerous during some winters than others. Can be seen in large numbers during fall and spring migration.

Almost always in groups of up to 10–25 birds, hunting in large open fields or prairies. Groups are mixed, consisting of adults and juveniles and light and dark morphs. Individuals try to steal from each other after one makes a kill. Monogamous, with pairs often staying together for life.

Has smaller, weaker feet than other raptors of similar size and must hunt smaller prey. Hunts from the air, often hovering, facing into a strong wind before diving for mice or voles. Will also perch in a tree or on a fence post to watch for prey when the wind is weak. Often feeds on the ground after catching prey. Perches on surprisingly thin branches at the top of small trees.

Northern Goshawk

Accipiter gentilis

YEAR-ROUND
WINTER

Family: Hawks, Eagles and Kites (Accipitridae)

Size: M 18–20" (45–50 cm); WS 3¼–3½' (1–1.1 m)
F 21–25" (53–64 cm); WS 3½–3¾' (1.1–1.14 m)

Weight: M 1½–1¾ lb. (.7–.8 kg); F 1¾–2 lb. (.8–.9 kg)

Male: A large hawk with a bluish gray back and upper wings. Light gray breast and belly with fine horizontal barring. Gray underwings with fine dark barring. Prominent white eyebrows (superciliary lines). Long gray tail with fluffy white undertail coverts. Black crown and line through the eyes. Deep red-to-mahogany eyes. Yellow feet.

Female: similar to male, noticeably larger, barring on the breast is more coarse

Juvenile: overall brown with vertical streaks on the chest, irregular dark bands on the tail, yellow eyes

Habitat: woodlands, forests, wooded backyards, parks

Food: small mammals (especially Snowshoe Hares), small and large birds (especially Ruffed Grouse)

Sounds: high-pitched repetitive "kee-kee-kee" similar to the call of the Cooper's Hawk (pg. 73) when intruders get near the nest

Compare: Larger than Cooper's Hawk (pg. 73), which lacks white superciliary lines and has a rusty chest. Much larger than Sharp-shinned Hawk (pg. 69), which has a rusty breast. Slightly smaller than the Gyrfalcon (pg. 57), which lacks the white line above each eye and has large markings on a white breast. Look for the gray breast and fluffy white undertail coverts to help identify the Northern Goshawk.

Flight: large-bodied hawk with very long, wide wings, rounded wing tips, short "fingertips" (primaries) and a long narrow tail; rapid, shallow wing beats interspersed with short gliding; typical accipiter flight

Migration: non-migrator to irruptive; moves out of the region in 10-year cycles; moves around during winter

Nesting: platform, in a mature tree in dense deciduous forest or coniferous woods, usually in the first fork or crotch of a tree, constructed with sticks, twigs and branches with evergreen needles attached; male and female repair an old nest or build a new one; 1 brood

Eggs/Incubation: 2–5 bluish white eggs, sometimes with brown markings; female does most of the incubating 36–38 days; male does the hunting and feeds the nesting female before and after the young hatch

Fledging: 35–42 days; female feeds the young; male does the hunting and brings food to the female, who feeds the chicks; upon leaving the nest (fledging), the young continue to beg for food, chasing parents around after they capture prey; chicks learn to hunt by watching and copying parental behavior and are hunting by the end of their first summer

Stan's Notes: The largest and most aggressive of the three woodland accipiters. Hunts by chasing or surprising prey. This hawk is extremely dependent on the Snowshoe Hare for food. Goshawk populations are known to follow hare populations, irrupting out of the normal range during the years when hare populations are low. This occurs in 10-year cycles. Also feeds on Ruffed Grouse as a secondary food source.

The smaller male is more agile than the female and hunts for smaller prey. The female hunts for larger prey. Female is very aggressive at the nest, boldly attacking intruders, even humans.

Usually starts to breed at 3 years of age. A small percentage will nest at 1–2 years of age without full adult plumage. During irruption years, juveniles migrate first, followed a couple weeks later by adults.

Eastern

Red-tailed Hawk

Buteo jamaicensis

YEAR-ROUND
SUMMER

Family: Hawks, Eagles and Kites (Accipitridae)

Size: M 18–22" (45–56 cm); WS 3¾–4¼' (1.14–1.3 m)
F 19–25" (48–64 cm); WS 4¼–4¾' (1.3–1.45 m)

Weight: M 1¾–2 lb. (.8–.9 kg); F 2–2½ lb. (.9–1.1 kg)

Male: Five varieties, from chocolate brown to nearly
all white. Overall brown with a lighter brown
head (sometimes blond), white chest and a distinctive brown belly band. White V on the back
(scapulars), seen when perched. Rusty red tail,
usually seen only from above. White underwings with a small dark patch on the leading
edge close to the shoulder (patagial). Heavy bill.
White chin. Brown eyes and bright yellow cere.

Female: same as male, noticeably larger

Juvenile: similar to adults, lacks the red tail, longer tail
with narrow light and dark tail bands, speckled
breast, dark belly band, light yellow eyes

Habitat: open fields, meadows, along highways, forests,
wooded backyards, parks, rural to urban areas

Food: small and medium-sized mammals, large birds,
snakes, fish, large insects, bats, carrion

Sounds: screams a long high-pitched call that falls in
pitch and intensity when interlopers get close to
the nest; young repeat a begging call for food

Compare: Red-shouldered Hawk (pg. 81) lacks a red tail and
white breast. Cooper's Hawk (pg. 73) is smaller, with shorter,
rounded wings.

Golden Eagle

Aquila chrysaetos

MIGRATION
SUMMER
WINTER

Family: Hawks, Eagles and Kites (Accipitridae)

Size: M 30–35" (76–88 cm); WS 6–6¾' (1.8–2.06 m)
F 34–37" (86–94 cm); WS 6¾–7¾' (2.06–2.36 m)

Weight: M 8–10 lb. (3.6–4.5 kg.); F 10–12 lb. (4.5–5.4 kg)

Male: A uniform dark brown body with a golden head and nape of neck. Gray bill with a dark tip and yellow around the base (cere). Brown leading half with gray trailing half of underwings, dark wing tips (primaries). Narrow gray tail bands with a wide dark terminal band. Yellow feet.

Female: similar to male, noticeably larger, with a wide, irregular gray band across the center of tail

Juvenile: white wrist patches and base of tail, nape is golden at all ages, long tail and wing feathers

Habitat: mountainous terrain, cliffs, valleys

Food: small to medium-large mammals, large birds, reptiles, large insects, carrion

Sounds: fairly quiet; can be vocal when one mate makes a kill and the other wants it; gives a high-pitched "yee-yee-yee" call; juveniles beg for food with a loud stuttering call

Compare: Similar size as the Bald Eagle (pg. 105), but lacks the white head and tail. Juvenile Golden Eagle, a large dark bird with consistent white markings on its wrists and base of tail, is often confused with juvenile Bald Eagle, which has inconsistent white markings all over its body and wings. Osprey (pg. 109) has a white body and dark wrist marks. The Turkey Vulture (pg. 117) is smaller, with two-toned wings and a shorter tail.

adult

juvenile

juvenile

Flight: slow, strong, shallow wing beats interspersed with long periods of gliding; holds wings flat (horizontally) to a slightly upturned angle (dihedral) while soaring

Migration: complete migrator, to southern states and Mexico or just moves around to find food; in the Northeast, most are seen during migration when they pass through; some remain along large rivers in the region

Nesting: massive platform, on a ledge of a cliff face, sometimes in a tree; female and male build, bringing in large branches and other new nesting material each season, increasing the size over the years; 1 brood

Eggs/Incubation: 1–2 white eggs with brown markings; female and male incubate 43–45 days; male does the most hunting and feeds the nesting female before and after the young hatch

Fledging: 63–75 days; female and male feed young; male does the majority of hunting and brings food to the female, who feeds the chicks; upon leaving the nest (fledging), the young continue to beg for food, following parents around after they capture prey; chicks learn to hunt by watching and copying parental behavior

Stan's Notes: Large and powerful raptor that has no trouble taking larger prey such as jackrabbits, foxes, squirrels, rabbits, young deer and marmots. Hunts by perching or soaring and watching for movement. Inhabits mountainous terrain and open areas, requiring large territories to provide ample food. Scavenges stillbirths and animals that died from winter kill.

Thought to mate for life, with pairs remaining together year-round, even migrating together. Renews its pair bond during late winter with spectacular high-flying courtship displays.

Usually nests on cliff faces. Uses a well-established nest that has been used for generations. Not uncommon for it to add things to the nest such as antlers, bones or barbed wire. New nests are just a smattering of sticks, but over the years as it adds new materials the nest can become up to 6 feet (1.8 m) tall.

Usually lays 2 eggs, with up to 3–4 days in between eggs. Young couples lay only 1 egg. Young eagles become independent of their parents by fall migration. The young take 6 years to obtain adult plumage, the same time that they start to breed.

Bald Eagle

Haliaeetus leucocephalus

YEAR-ROUND
MIGRATION
SUMMER
WINTER

Family: Hawks, Eagles and Kites (Accipitridae)

Size: M 31–35" (79–88 cm); WS 6–6¾' (1.8–2.06 m)
F 35–37" (88–94 cm); WS 6¾–8' (2.06–2.4 m)

Weight: M 8–10 lb. (3.6–4.5 kg); F 10–12 lb. (4.5–5.4 kg)

Male: Dark brown body and wings with a white head and tail. Large, curving yellow bill. Yellow feet. Long broad wings with well-defined individual primary feathers at the tip of wings.

Female: same as male, noticeably larger

Juvenile: first year has a very dark head, bill, body, wings, white wing linings; second through fourth years have a brown head covered with white speckles, body and wings spotted with white, dark-tipped gray bill, long tail and wings, appearing larger than adults; white head and tail at 4-6 years

Habitat: lakes, rivers, reservoirs, most large permanent water sources

Food: fish, carrion, birds (mainly ducks)

Sounds: very vocal in all seasons; gives a wide variety of calls, all short, shrill, high-pitched whistles, often ascending in pitch and repeated over and over

Compare: Golden Eagle (pg. 101) is similar in size, but has a golden nape and lacks the white head and tail of the adult Bald Eagle. Juvenile Golden has consistent white marks on its wrists (carpals) and base of tail, with a black terminal tail band; juvenile Bald has inconsistent white marks over its body and wings. Osprey (pg. 109) has a white body and dark wrist marks. Turkey Vulture (pg. 117) has two-toned wings and a shorter tail.

Flight: long broad wings tipped with well-defined individual primary feathers; slow, shallow wing beats; holds wings flat (horizontally) while soaring

Migration: complete to non-migrator, with many moving to southern states; many remain, congregating at open water sources to fish; moves around to find food during winter

Nesting: massive platform, usually in a tree; female and male build, bringing in new nesting material each season; 1 brood

Eggs/Incubation: 2–3 off-white eggs; female and male incubate 34–36 days; male does the most hunting and feeds the nesting female before and after the young hatch

Fledging: 75–90 days; female and male feed young; male does the majority of hunting and brings food to the female, who feeds the chicks; upon leaving the nest (fledging), young still beg for food, chasing parents around after they capture prey; chicks learn to hunt by watching the behavior of their parents

Stan's Notes: Driven to near extinction due to DDT poisoning and illegal killing. Now doing well across North America.

Like other raptors, eagles have 10 primary flight feathers, with 17 secondary flight feathers—4 more than other raptors. Adults acquire adult plumage at 4–6 years. Some retain their juvenile head plumage until 8 years. Younger juveniles have longer tail and wing feathers, up to 2 inches (5 cm), making them look larger than adults. Sometimes Bald juveniles are confused with Golden Eagles (pg. 101) due to their similar color and size.

In the midair mating ritual, one eagle will flip upside down and lock talons with another. Both tumble, then break apart to continue flight. Thought to mate for life, but will switch mates if not successful reproducing or if one mate dies. Returns to the same nest each year, adding more sticks, enlarging it to massive proportions, at times up to 1,000 pounds (450 kg).

Eagles in northern latitudes are much larger than those in southern latitudes. Alaskan eagles are particularly large, while those in Florida are the smallest. Northern males are larger than southern females. Southern eagles can be up to 7 inches (18 cm) smaller than northern eagles of the same sex.

Osprey

Pandion haliaetus

SUMMER

Family: Osprey (Pandionidae)

Size: L 21–24" (53–61 cm); WS 5–5½' (1.5–1.7 m)

Weight: 2⅛–4⅛ lb. (1–1.9 kg)

Male: Large eagle-like raptor with a white breast and belly and nearly black back. Dark bill. White head, sometimes with a dark forehead. Dark line through the eyes (auricular), extending to the back of head. Pale yellow eyes. Long wings with black wrist (carpal) patches and tips of the primaries. White body and axillaries. Two-toned wings, white leading, dark trailing. Gray feet.

Female: similar to male, slightly larger, often has a necklace of brown streaks on the breast; necklace is unreliable for female identification

Juvenile: similar to adults, with a tan-to-rust breast and wing linings, orange eyes (Jun-Jan); appears like an adult by 1 year of age

Habitat: lakes, rivers, reservoirs, most large permanent water sources

Food: primarily live fish; sometimes will eat dead fish, reptiles, amphibians and small waterfowl

Sounds: very vocal in all seasons; gives a wide variety of calls, each a short high-pitched shrill or whistle, often ascending in pitch, repeated over and over

Compare: Bald Eagle (pg. 105) has an all-white head and tail and a large yellow bill. Juvenile Bald Eagle is brown with white speckles, lacking a white body. Look for a white belly, dark eye stripe and black carpal patches to identify the Osprey.

juvenile

juvenile

adult fishing

Flight: long narrow wings, cupped or bowed downward and angled (crooked) backward, often appearing swept back or in an M shape when in flight; fast, shallow wing beats; hovers before diving

Migration: complete migrator, to Florida and other southern states, Mexico, Central and South America; during migration to South America, follows land masses or crosses large bodies of water such as the Gulf of Mexico; migrates alone during the day

Nesting: platform, often on a man-made tower equipped with a wooden platform, large light posts, bridges, buoys, other human structures, occasionally in tall trees; female and male build, bringing in new nesting material each season; 1 brood

Eggs/Incubation: 2–4 white eggs with brown marks; female and male incubate 32–42 days; male does the most hunting and feeds the nesting female before and after the young hatch

Fledging: 48–58 days; male and female feed young; male does the majority of hunting and brings fish to the female, who feeds the chicks; upon leaving the nest (fledging), the young continue to beg for food, chasing parents after they catch a fish; chicks learn to fish by watching and copying parental behavior

Stan's Notes: The only species in its family. Neither a hawk nor an eagle, it has unique feet, with two toes that face forward and two backward, unlike the feet of hawks and eagles, which have three forward and one backward. It is also the only raptor that plunges into water feet first, often completely submerging to catch fish. Hunts from heights of up to 100 feet (30 m). Often hovers for a few seconds before diving. Can take off from the water's surface while carrying fish. Carries a fish in a head-first position for better aerodynamics. Often forced by Bald Eagles (pg. 105) to drop its catch, which eagles snatch and eat.

Also known as Fish Hawk, feeding mostly on live fish. Nearly always seen in association with water. Some Ospreys are comfortable having people around their nests. Others are shy. Most don't try to nest until they are at least 3 years old. Young return to the nest each night after fledging, unlike other raptors.

Can live up to 20–25 years. Recent studies show Ospreys mate perhaps for life or until one dies, after which the survivor takes a new mate. Courtship includes high circling and vocalizations by both members, with the male hovering in flight. Mated pairs do not migrate together or go to the same wintering grounds.

Black Vulture

Coragyps atratus

AR-ROUND

Family: Vultures (Cathartidae)

Size: L 25–28" (64–71 cm); WS 4½–5¼' (1.4–1.6 m)

Weight: 4–5 lb. (1.8–2.3 kg)

Male: All-black bird with a dark gray wrinkled head and gray legs. Short square tail. During flight, all-black body and wings, with light gray wing tips (primaries). Long broad wings with well-defined primary feathers.

Female: same as male

Juvenile: similar to adults, with unwrinkled black skin on head

Habitat: open country, farm fields, woodlands, along highways, close to rivers, lakes, creeks and other permanent water sources

Food: carrion, just about any dead animal of any size, occasionally capturing small live mammals and birds; also known to eat vegetables and plants; parents regurgitate for young

Sounds: mostly mute; hisses, grunts and groans

Compare: Slightly smaller than the Turkey Vulture (pg. 117) and lacking the bright red head. Turkey Vulture has two-toned wings, a black leading edge and light gray trailing edge. Black Vulture has shorter gray-tipped wings and a shorter tail than the Turkey Vulture. Adult and juvenile Bald Eagles (pg. 105) are larger and lack the two-toned wings of Black Vulture.

juvenile

juvenile

Flight: short, wide black wings with gray tips (primaries), holding wings at a slight upsweep and also flat; fast, flicking wing beats followed by gliding; teeters back and forth in air currents during flight

Migration: non-migrator to partial, moving just far enough south to survive winter; moves around to find food

Nesting: no nest, or minimal nest on the ground under thick vegetation, in a protected cliff, cave or broken-off tree trunk, on the first floor of an abandoned building; 1 brood

Eggs/Incubation: 1–3 light green eggs with dark markings; female and male incubate 37–45 days; male forages much more than the female and feeds her before and after the young hatch

Fledging: 75–80 days; female and male feed young; nestlings and fledglings are fed regurgitated food by both parents; upon leaving the nest (fledging), young follow their parents, hissing and grunting for food; chicks watch the parents and learn to forage for food; young remain with adults until the first winter

Stan's Notes: Also called Black Buzzard. The only member of its genus, *Coragyps*. Holds its wings straight out to the sides with wing tips curved up during flight. This is unlike Turkey Vulture (pg. 117), which holds its wings in a slight V shape.

Prefers fresh carrion, but also feeds on decaying meat. Seems to be less skilled at finding carrion, often following Turkey Vultures to find food. Sense of smell is believed to be less developed than in Turkey Vultures; some think the Black has no sense of smell. More aggressive than Turkey Vultures while feeding, with many fights and squabbles. When startled, regurgitates powerfully and accurately onto the intruder, especially while defending the nest.

More gregarious than Turkey Vulture, often nesting and roosting with other Black Vultures, especially after breeding season. Families stay together for up to a year. It is thought a male and female will mate for life. Often seen in groups at watering holes, drinking freely and bathing regularly. Pairs preen each other; some individuals preen other bird species.

Has moved farther north in recent years, where new records are reported often. Moves out of northern ranges in fall. Does not migrate in southern states. Range extends south into Chile.

YEAR-ROUND
SUMMER

Turkey Vulture

Cathartes aura

Family: Vultures (Cathartidae)

Size: L 26–32" (66–80 cm); WS 5½–6' (1.7–1.8 m)

Weight: 3–4 lb. (1.4–1.8 kg)

Male: Dark brown-to-black plumage. Naked red head. Wings look two-toned during flight, with dark underwing coverts and a gray trailing edge and tip. Wing tips (primaries) end in finger-like projections. Long tail. Hooked ivory bill. Reddish legs and feet, usually stained with some tan to off-white.

Female: same as male, slightly smaller

Juvenile: similar to adults, with a gray-to-black head and bill

Habitat: open country, farm fields, woodlands, along highways, close to rivers, lakes, creeks and other permanent water sources

Food: carrion, just about any dead animal of any size; parents regurgitate for young

Sounds: mostly mute; hisses, grunts and groans; young grunt to beg for food

Compare: Black Vulture (pg. 113) has shorter wings and a short square tail. Adult and juvenile Bald Eagles (pg. 105) are larger and lack Turkey Vulture's two-toned wings. Unlike the Black Vulture and Bald Eagle, the Turkey Vulture holds its wings in a shallow V shape during flight and tilts back and forth from wing tip to wing tip. Look for the two-toned wings while the Turkey Vulture is soaring to help identify.

adult

juvenile

standing on prey

Flight: very wide and relatively long wings for such a small raptor; buoyant flight with fluttering wing beats; flies silently

Migration: partial to non-migrator to complete; moves as much as several hundred miles south of breeding grounds in the fall; will remain all winter in one location

Nesting: cavity, former woodpecker cavity, wooden nest box; does not add any nesting material; 1 brood

Eggs/Incubation: 5–6 white eggs; female and male incubate 26–28 days; male does the most hunting and feeds the nesting female before and after the young hatch

Fledging: 27–34 days; male and female feed young; male does the majority of hunting and brings food to the female, who feeds the chicks; upon leaving the nest (fledging), the young continue to beg for food, following parents around after they capture prey; chicks learn to hunt by watching and copying the behavior of their parents

Stan's Notes: Our smallest owl, but not often recognized as an owl because of its diminutive size. The common name "Saw-whet" was given for its raspy whistling call, which sounds like a saw blade being sharpened.

A resident of the Northeast, well known for its annual autumn migration, moving south into other parts of the region. Large numbers of these owls migrate consistently to areas south of their breeding range and return in the spring.

Usually found in mixed forests, roosting in cavities, conifers or thick vegetation. Can be tame and approachable, especially during winter, when it often roosts in thick coniferous hedges.

Well-developed fringe and down pile on primary flight feathers result in silent flight. Strictly a nighttime hunter. Eats mainly mice, regardless of the time of year. Will often catch a mouse during the night, return to its daytime roost and stand on its prey until the following evening before dining. Sits on frozen prey to thaw it before eating.

Young hatch asynchronously. The youngest often perishes when the older owlets fledge, leaving it behind without parental care. Known to nest in Wood Duck boxes put up by landowners.

Boreal Owl

Aegolius funereus

Family: Owls (Strigidae)

Size: L 9–11" (23–28 cm); WS 17–21" (43–53 cm)

Weight: 4–6 oz. (113–170 g)

Male: Small brown-to-gray non-eared owl with white spots on the back and wings. White spots and streaks on the breast and belly. Large fluffy head and obvious white facial disk outlined in black. Bright yellow eyes. Small dull yellow bill.

Female: same as male, slightly larger

Juvenile: dark gray to nearly black with prominent white eyebrows and chin and several white spots on the wings

Habitat: mixed coniferous and deciduous forests

Food: mainly voles, other small animals such as mice, occasionally birds

Sounds: series of up to 10 low "toots" within 2–3 seconds, repeated over and over

Compare: The Northern Saw-whet Owl (pg. 121) is more common and slightly smaller than the Boreal Owl, with a streaked breast and lacking dark outlining around its facial disk. Eastern Screech-Owl (pg. 125) is smaller, has ear tufts and lacks the white face.

adult hunting

juvenile

Flight: broad round wings; shallow, rapid wing beats and silent flight; short periods of gliding before landing

Migration: non-migrator to irruptive, moving out of normal range in some winters to search for food; can be seen during some winters, but absent during most; very uncommon owl in the Northeast

Nesting: cavity, natural hole in a tree, old woodpecker cavity, will accept a man-made wooden box, may use the same cavity for many years; does not add any nesting material; 1 brood

Eggs/Incubation: 4–6 white eggs; female incubates 27–28 days; male does the hunting and feeds the nesting female from about 1 week before laying eggs until 3 weeks after the young hatch; young hatch asynchronously

Fledging: 28–33 days; male and female feed young; male does the majority of hunting and brings food to the female, who feeds the chicks; upon leaving the nest (fledging), the young continue to beg for food, following parents after they capture prey; chicks learn to hunt by watching and copying parents

Stan's Notes: This owl irrupts out of its normal range during winters with limited food supply. Generally, females and young move in irruption years. Usually seen only when hunting for mice along roads or in yards by bird feeders. Caches food in crevices, tree forks or other small places. Sits on frozen prey to thaw it before eating. Too small to penetrate deep snow to get prey; many starve to death in winter when snow is several feet deep. Often tame, not responding to the presence of people.

An efficient predator and stealthy flier. Silent flight is due to a well-developed fringe and down pile on its flight feathers. Even with all of these advantages, it still is a sit-and-wait hunter.

Named "Boreal" for its nesting habitat in coniferous or boreal forests. Experiences wide population swings in different regions. Some individuals can be seen in some years; in others, they are nonexistent. The male establishes a territory in spring and begins to call. When a female is attracted and flies into the territory, the male will fly to a possible nest cavity and continue to call. Retrieving a cached item of food, the male will present it to the female to show that he is a good provider.

AR-ROUND

Northern Hawk Owl

Surnia ulula

Family: Owls (Strigidae)

Size: L 14–17" (36–43 cm); WS 28–33" (71–84 cm)

Weight: 10–13 oz. (284–369 g)

Male: Overall dark brown to dark gray. Head is small compared with its body. White face outlined in black, with white speckles on the forehead. Flat, broad top of head. Many fine, rusty horizontal bars from breast to tail. Bright yellow eyes and yellow bill. Long, narrow pointed tail.

Female: same as male, slightly larger

Juvenile: light gray with a dark face, yellow eyes

Habitat: mixed coniferous and deciduous forests, dense woodlands, aspen parklands, along roadsides

Food: mice, voles and other small mammals, small birds, occasional insects

Sounds: series of high-pitched toots or whistles, repeated rapidly and typically at night during breeding season; female and juvenile give a soft screech

Compare: Much larger than the Boreal Owl (pg. 129), which has a brown and white breast and lacks the rusty horizontal barring of the Hawk Owl. Smaller than Barred Owl (pg. 149), which has dark eyes. Short-eared Owl (pg. 141) shares the same size, but Hawk Owl has a smaller head and longer tail. Look for the powerful hawk-like flight and swooping approach before landing to help identify the Northern Hawk Owl.

adult

adult dorsal

adult

adult
hawk-like flight

juvenile

Flight: long narrow wings with pointed tips; fast, stiff, wing beats with a powerful hawk-like flight and swooping approach before landing; during flight, wings crook backward at the wrist; sometimes flies close to the ground and swoops upward sharply to perch on a pole or tree; able to hover

Migration: non-migrator to irruptive; moves out of Canada in some winters to find food; not consistent from year to year, with only a handful showing up during some winters

138

Nesting: cavity, in a natural cavity in a tree, will use a nest box on a tree, sometimes nests on top of a stump; will also use a platform nest, taking an old nest of a crow or raven; does not add any nesting material; 1 brood

Eggs/Incubation: 5–7 white eggs; female incubates 25–30 days; male does the most hunting and feeds the nesting female before and after the young hatch

Fledging: 25–35 days; male and female feed young; male does the most hunting and brings food to the female, who feeds the chicks; upon leaving the nest (fledging), the young still beg for food, following the parents after they capture prey; chicks learn to hunt by watching their parents, staying with them until the following spring when the adults prepare to nest again

Stan's Notes: A uniquely shaped owl that flies like a hawk, with fast, stiff wing beats and pointed wings like a falcon. In fact, it was given the common name "Hawk" for the way it flies.

Frequently sits and covers its feet while perching, creating the appearance of a round feathery ball with a tail balancing on top of a branch or stick. Usually not afraid of people and often hunts during the daytime. Hunts with its eyesight and hearing, like other owl species. Often will hunt along roads, where an abundance of small rodents can be found. Caches extra mice and voles behind flaking bark and in forks of trees for later consumption. Clutch size in spring depends on the abundance of food during late winter.

Well known for its irruptive behavior in winter. Irruption can involve dozens to hundreds of owls moving usually south of their normal range to areas where they are not normally found to look for food. Not very common in the Northeast.

Short-eared Owl
Asio flammeus

Family: Owls (Strigidae)

Size: L 14–17" (36–43 cm); WS 3–3¼' (.9–1 m)

Weight: 11–12 oz. (312–340 g)

Male: Overall brown-to-tan plumage. Heavy streaks on the breast, with a lighter belly and spotted back. Very short, tiny ear tufts, usually not noticeable. Long wide wings with a distinctive black wrist (carpal) mark beneath and prominent tan patch near the upper end (primaries), with black tips. Dark patches around bright yellow eyes. Large head and short neck.

Female: same as male, overall darker with a darker face

Juvenile: similar to adults, light tan with a dark face

Habitat: open fields, meadows, marshes, prairies

Food: small mammals, birds

Sounds: harsh hissing any time of year; calls a soft "poo-poo-poo" during breeding season; female call is more quiet than the male and juvenile call is hoarser; gives an alarm bark; claps wings during flight, sounding like a whip cracking

Compare: Long-eared Owl (pg. 133) is about the same size, but it has long ear tufts and a rusty red face. Northern Harrier (pg. 85) has a similar flight pattern, but the males are all white underneath with black wing tips; female Harries are rust brown and lack the dark mask around the eyes.

adult

adult at nest

hunting

Flight: long wide wings; long, slow, stiff wing beats and erratic flight, distinctive and buoyant, like that of a butterfly; floats on air with wings outstretched, sometimes hovering above prey before dropping to the ground; occasionally swoops and claps wings together underneath the body while in flight, creating a whip-cracking sound

Migration: complete to partial migrator, moving south through the Northeast during winter; stays all year in some parts of the region

Nesting: ground nest, well concealed in thick vegetation and made with a loose gathering of dried grass; 1 brood

Eggs/Incubation: 4–7 white eggs; female incubates 26–30 days; male does the most hunting and feeds the nesting female before and after the young hatch

Fledging: 23–36 days; male and female feed young; male does the majority of hunting, both parents bring food and feed young; upon leaving the nest (fledging), the young continue to beg for food, at first waiting for the parents to bring food, then following them around to be fed; chicks learn to hunt by watching and copying the behavior of their parents

Stan's Notes: An owl of Alaska and northern Canada. Also found throughout western states. Seen mostly in the Northeast during migration and winter, when moving south. Often up to a dozen Shorties take up winter residency in large open areas and remain there all winter to hunt. Can be common in some years, nonexistent in others.

Main diet consists of small rodents such as voles and mice. Hunts over open fields, like Long-eared Owls (pg. 133), often floating on air just before dropping onto prey. Frequently starts to hunt 30 minutes to an hour before sunset. Hunts during the day when weather is overcast, making it one of the few owls you can see during the day. Look for the dark mask "mascara" around the eyes to help identify. Ear tufts are very short and hard to see unless the owl is perched and in alert posture.

Coughs up pellets in the same way as other owls. Owl pellets contain the undigested parts of prey such as bones and fur. Look for pellets below favorite perches.

Will perch on small trees out in the open to survey the area. Also sits on branches or fence posts to feed. At the nest, adults perform distraction displays to lure intruders away from the site. Sometimes nesting is semicolonial.

male

Barn Owl

Tyto alba

AR-ROUND
GRATION
UMMER

Family: Owls (Tytonidae)

Size: L 16–19" (40–48 cm); WS 3–3½' (.9–1.1 m)

Weight: 1–1¼ lb. (.5–.6 kg)

Male: A non-eared owl. Rusty tan on the back of head, back, wings and tail. Heart-shaped white facial disk, outlined in darker rusty brown. White breast and belly with many scattered tiny dark marks. Dark eyes. Long gray legs and gray feet. Ivory bill. White wing linings.

Female: slightly larger than male, with a rusty wash over a spotted breast and belly

Juvenile: fuzzy-looking with light gray-to-white plumage and a distinct heart-shaped face

Habitat: farm fields, woods, cliffs, semi-wooded areas, suburban areas, prairies

Food: mice and other small animals, birds, snakes

Sounds: harsh hissing any time of year; female call is more quiet than the male; juvenile call is hoarser

Compare: Easily identified by the white heart-shaped facial disk and dark eyes. The Snowy Owl (pg. 157) is much larger, has white plumage and lacks a heart-shaped face. Slightly larger than Short-eared Owl (pg. 141), which has a streaked chest and belly, dark marks around each eye and a less defined facial disk.

Barred Owl

Bubo varia

AR-ROUND

Family: Owls (Strigidae)

Size: L 20–24" (50–61 cm); WS 3–3½' (.9–1.1 m)

Weight: 1½–2 lb. (.7–.9 kg)

Male: Robust brown and gray owl with a large head, gray face, dark brown eyes and horizontal dark barring on the upper chest. Vertical streaks on the lower chest and belly. Yellow bill and feet. No ear tuft "horns."

Female: same as male, slightly larger

Juvenile: light gray with a black face, yellow bill

Habitat: forests, dense woodlands, wooded backyards, near lakes and streams

Food: mice, rabbits, other small to medium animals, small birds, fish, reptiles, amphibians

Sounds: extremely vocal in all seasons and makes many strange sounds; calls 6–8 hoots that sound like "who-who-who-cooks-for-you"; also barks, hisses and gives wheezy, raspy calls repeatedly; female voice is higher than the male; juvenile gives a hissing call when begging for food; day-time calling summons the mate to the nest

Compare: Lacks the "horns" of Great Horned Owl (pg. 153) and ear tufts of the tiny Eastern Screech-Owl (pg. 125). Eastern Screech-Owl is less than half the size of Barred Owl. Smaller than the Great Gray Owl (pg. 161), which has yellow eyes. Look for the dark eyes to help identify the Barred Owl.

adult
hunting

juvenile

Flight: short broad wings with a wide round tip; slow, deep, full wing beats with much gliding; flies silently

Migration: non-migrator; will move around to find food or establish new territories during winter

Nesting: cavity, large natural hole in a mature tree, cavity must be large enough for an adult and 2–3 young, sometimes uses the same tree cavity for many years; does not add any nesting material; 1 brood

Eggs/Incubation: 2–3 white eggs; female incubates 28–33 days; male does the most hunting and feeds the nesting female before and after the young hatch

Fledging: 42–44 days; female and male feed young; male does the most hunting and brings food to the female, who usually feeds the chicks; males may also sometimes feed chicks before they reach 2 weeks of age; upon leaving the nest (fledging), the young continue to beg for food, chasing parents around after they capture prey; chicks learn to hunt by copying parental behavior; parents feed the young for up to 4 months after they fledge, usually until the end of their first summer; young in a small cavity tend to fledge sooner than those in a large cavity

Stan's Notes: A very common owl in the Northeast. Often can be seen hunting during the day, watching for mice, birds and other prey. Not easily frightened away from the daytime roost. Often mobbed by crows. One of the few owls to take fish from a lake or stream. Sits on a branch over the water, watching for fish. Drops down and hovers briefly with several deep wing beats while reaching its feet into the water to snatch a fish.

Prefers dense deciduous woodlands with sparse undergrowth. Might be easy to miss on a tree branch due to the camouflage of its brown-to-gray feathers. Can be attracted with a simple large nest box that has a large opening, attached to a tree. Known to drink and bathe in birdbaths or water puddles.

Entertains people in the area with raucous calls in the evening or during the day. Often sounds like a dog barking just before giving its call of 6–8 hoots. The Great Horned Owl (pg. 153) hoot call differs, sounding like "hoo-hoo-hoo-hoooo."

adult landing

juvenile

Flight: long broad wings, cupped or bowed downward during flight; slow, shallow wing beats; silent flight

Migration: non-migrator; moves around in search of food or to establish new territories during winter

Nesting: no nest; takes over the nest of a crow, heron or hawk or uses a partial cavity, stump or broken-off tree; 1 brood

Eggs/Incubation: 2–3 white eggs; female incubates 26–30 days; male does the most hunting and feeds the nesting female before and after the young hatch

Fledging: 30–35 days; male and female feed young; male does the majority of the hunting and brings food to the female, who feeds the chicks; upon leaving the nest (fledging), young still beg for food, chasing parents after they catch prey; chicks learn to hunt by copying their parents' behavior, staying with them until the following winter, when the adults prepare for nesting

Stan's Notes: One of the most common owls in the Northeast. Often in backyards. The first bird to nest each season. Starts to mate and lay eggs in late January to March across the region. When the first egg is laid, the female must remain on the nest to keep the eggs from freezing. The male stands by to sit on the eggs while the female takes a few breaks each day. Aside from this, the female incubates the eggs full-time for nearly a month. Afterward, she sits on her newly hatched chicks (brood) for up to 10 days. Once the chicks get well-developed downy feathers and can control their body temperature, they are left unattended for short periods. Mating starts at 2–3 years. Life span in the wild is 20–25 years.

Able to hear a mouse move under a foot of snow. Can pinpoint prey in total darkness. One of the few fearless animals that kills skunks and porcupines. Also called Flying Tiger. Flight feather tips are ragged, resulting in air turbulence reduction and silent flight. Feathery tufts ("horns") on head have nothing to do with hearing; may help to blend its body into the environment. Can lay the tufts down flat, or hold them up when alert or startled. The neck has 14 vertebrae, enabling the head to swivel up to 280 degrees; the head cannot turn all the way around. Eyelids close from the top down, like those of people.

male

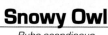

Snowy Owl

Bubo scandiacus

WINTER

Family: Owls (Strigidae)

Size: M 20–24" (50–61 cm); WS 4½–5' (1.4–1.5 m)
F 23–26" (58–66 cm); WS 5–5½' (1.5–1.7 m)

Weight: M 2½–3½ lb. (1.1–1.6 kg); F 4–4½ lb. (1.8–2 kg)

Male: Nearly pure white with a relatively small round head, bright yellow eyes and small dark bill. Varying amounts of small dark markings all over the back and wings. Feet are completely covered with white feathers.

Female: noticeably larger than the male, with many dark bars overall, especially on the top of head, back and wings

Juvenile: similar to the adult female, with dark horizontal bars and a white face; the younger the juvenile, the more barring

Habitat: bogs, meadows, mixed forests, farm fields, airports, frozen lakes or bays during winter, tundra

Food: small and medium-large animals such as mice, lemmings, voles, rabbits and hares, birds

Sounds: normally quiet except during breeding season; gives a high-pitched whistle and growling bark during territorial squabbles or food fights; will repeat a muffled hoot during breeding season

Compare: Our only white owl, rarely confused with any other bird of prey. Slightly larger than Great Horned Owl (pg. 153) which is much darker and has ear tufts. Shorter than the Great Gray Owl (pg. 161), which has a much larger head and is gray. Larger than white morph Gyrfalcon (pg. 57), which has a tiny head and eyes on the sides of its head.

Great Gray Owl

Strix nebulosa

WINTER

Family: Owls (Strigidae)

Size: L 24–29" (61–74 cm); WS 4–4½' (1.2–1.4 m)

Weight: 2–2½ lb. (.9–1.1 kg)

Male: Large gray owl with a puffy-looking round head. Large, round, light gray facial disk outlined with a thin black line. Yellow eyes. Eye size is similar to that in other large owls, but they appear tiny because of the large head and huge facial disk. Black and white throat, resembling a bow tie. Dense layer of feathers covering legs and feet.

Female: same as male, slightly larger

Juvenile: similar to adults, light gray with a dark face

Habitat: northern coniferous and deciduous forests, aspen parklands, open woodlands, along roads

Food: small to medium mammals such as mice, voles and shrews

Sounds: typically quiet except during breeding season; repeats 5–10 deep huffing hoots at regular intervals; female responds with a low whistle or hoot; juveniles usually don't vocalize

Compare: Barred Owl (pg. 149) is smaller and has dark eyes. Great Horned Owl (pg. 153) is smaller and has ear tufts. Snowy Owl (pg. 157) is nearly all white.

HELPFUL RESOURCES

Cornell Lab of Ornithology Handbook of Bird Biology, Second Edition. Edited by Sandy Podulka, Ronald W. Rohrbaugh Jr. and Rick Bonney. Princeton, NJ: Princeton University Press, 2004.

Field Guide to Hawks of North America, Second Edition, A. Clark, William S. and Brian K. Wheeler. Boston, MA: Houghton Mifflin, 2001.

Hawks in Flight: The Flight Identification of North American Migrant Raptors. Dunne, Peter, David Allen Sibley and Clay Sutton. Boston, MA: Houghton Mifflin, 1989.

Manual of Ornithology: Avian Structure and Function. Proctor, Noble S. and Patrick J. Lynch. New Haven, CT: Yale University Press, 1998.

North American Owls: Biology and Natural History, Second Edition. Johnsgard, Paul A. Washington, DC: Smithsonian Institution, 2002.

Ornithology, Third Edition. Gill, Frank B. New York, NY: W. H. Freeman and Company, 2006.

Owls of the United States and Canada: A Complete Guide to Their Biology and Behavior. Lynch, Wayne. Baltimore, MD: The Johns Hopkins University Press, 2007.

Owls of the World: Their Lives, Behavior and Survival. Duncan, Dr. James R. Toronto, ON: Firefly Books, 2003.

Photographic Guide to North American Raptors, A. Wheeler, Brian K. and William S. Clark. New York, NY: Academic Press, 1999.

Raptors: North American Birds of Prey. Snyder, Noel F. R. and Helen Snyder. Stillwater, MN: Voyageur Press, 1997.

Raptors of Eastern North America: The Wheeler Guides. Wheeler, Brian K. Princeton, NJ: Princeton University Press, 2003.

Sibley Guide to Birds, The. Sibley, David Allen. New York, NY: Alfred A. Knopf, 2000.

Emergency

Injured raptors should be turned over to a licensed wildlife rehabilitator. Check local listings for a rehabilitator near you.

Web Pages

The internet is a valuable place to learn more about raptors. You may find studying raptors on the net a fun way to discover additional information about them or to spend a long winter night. These websites will assist you in your pursuit of raptors. If a web address doesn't work (they often change a bit), just enter the name of the group into a search engine to track down the new web address.

Site	Address
Cape May Bird Observatory	www.birdcapemay.org
Hawk Mountain	www.hawkmountain.org
American Birding Association	www.americanbirding.org
Cornell Lab of Ornithology	www.birds.cornell.edu
Author Stan Tekiela's home page	www.naturesmart.com

CHECKLIST/INDEX

Use the boxes to check the raptors you've seen.

PHOTO CREDITS

All photos are copyright of their respective photographers.

Deborah Allen: 110 (juvenile perching)

Doug Backlund: 134 (juvenile)

Tony Beck: 58 (adult dark)

Rick and Nora Bowers: 98 (adult Eastern flight), 114 (juvenile flight), 138 (juvenile), 162 (juvenile)

Michael Brown: 82 (adult dorsal)

Marshall J. Iliff: 122 (adult flight)

Kevin T. Karlson: 46 (top male flight), 114 (main)

Tony Leukering: 78 (adult dark)

Maslowski Wildlife Productions: 126 (adult gray)

Jake Paredes: 66 (juvenile perching)

Stephen J. Shaluta Jr./Dembinsky Photo Associates: 144

Brian E. Small: 134 (main)

Dick Stilwell: 66 (adult perching)

Ted Swem: 58 (juvenile gray), 122 (juvenile), 130 (juvenile), 158 (juvenile)

Stan Tekiela: 14 (both), 15 (both), 44, 46 (main), 50 (main, adult flight), 52, 54 (all except juvenile flight), 56, 58 (main, adult white, chicks), 60, 62 (all except adult dorsal), 66 (main), 70 (all insets), 72, 74 (main, top adult flight), 76, 78 (main, top adult flight, both juvenile insets), 80, 82 (all except juvenile insets), 84, 86 (male flight, female flight), 88, 90 (all insets except adult dark), 92, 94 (all except adult dorsal), 96, 98 (main, adult Harlan's, adult Krider's perching, all juvenile insets), 100, 102 (main, adult flight), 104, 106 (all), 108, 110 (main, fishing), 112, 116, 118 (both insets), 120, 122 (main),

124, 126 (main, juvenile gray), 128, 130 (main, adult hunting), 132, 134 (all insets except juvenile), 136, 138 (all except juvenile), 140, 142 (main, adult at nest), 146 (all), 148, 150 (main, juvenile), 152, 154 (all), 156, 158 (main), 160, 162 (both flight)

Brian K. Wheeler: 46 (male juvenile), 50 (both juvenile insets), 54 (juvenile flight), 64, 66 (juvenile flight), 78 (adult dorsal), 86 (main, juvenile perching), 90 (main, adult dark), 98 (adult Krider's flight), 102 (both juvenile insets), 110 (juvenile flight), 114 (juvenile perching), 118 (main)

Jim Zipp: 46 (male diving, female flight), 48, 68, 70 (main), 74 (adult dorsal, all juvenile insets), 82 (both juvenile insets), 86 (juvenile flight), 94 (adult dorsal), 142 (adult flight inset), 150 (adult hunting), 158 (adult dorsal)

To the best of the publisher's knowledge, all photos were of live raptors. Some photos were taken under controlled conditions.

ABOUT THE AUTHOR

Naturalist, wildlife photographer and writer Stan Tekiela is the originator of the popular state-specific field guide series that includes *Birds of Connecticut Field Guide, Birds of Maryland & Delaware Field Guide, Birds of New York Field Guide* and *Birds of Pennsylvania Field Guide.* For over two decades, Stan has authored more than 100 field guides, nature appreciation books and wildlife audio CDs for nearly every state in the nation, presenting many species of birds, mammals, reptiles and amphibians, trees, wildflowers and cacti. Holding a Bachelor of Science degree in Natural History from the University of Minnesota and as an active professional naturalist for more than 20 years, Stan studies and photographs wildlife throughout the United States and has received various national and regional awards for his books and photographs. Also a well-known columnist and radio personality, his syndicated column appears in more than 20 newspapers and his wildlife programs are broadcast on a number of Midwest radio stations. He is a member of the North American Nature Photography Association and Canon Professional Services. Stan resides in Victoria, Minnesota, with his wife, Katherine, and daughter, Abigail. He can be contacted via his web page at www.naturesmart.com.

Identifying birds of prey is easier than ever!

With this book, watching raptors is more enjoyable, informative and productive.

- **Only Northeast birds of prey** – all of the hawks, eagles, falcons, kites, vultures and owls found in the Northeast

- **Organized for efficient use** – species organized by group, then size from smallest to largest

- **Fact-filled information** – accessible for beginners but informative for more experienced birders

- **Stunning photos** – professional-quality sharpness and detail

- **Stan's Notes** – naturalist information and interesting gee-whiz facts not found in other guides

- **Quick-Compare section** – sketches, silhouettes and photos for side-by-side comparisons

About the Author

Stan Tekiela is a naturalist, wildlife photographer and the originator of many popular state-specific field guides. He has authored more than 100 field guides, nature books and audio CDs, presenting many species of birds, mammals, reptiles and amphibians, trees, wildflowers and cacti.

$14.95

adventure PUBLICATIONS

Adventure Publications, Inc.
820 Cleveland Street South
Cambridge, MN 55008
1-800-678-7006
www.adventurepublications.net
ISBN: 978-1-59193-316-8

ISBN 1-59193-316-1

5 1495

9 781591 933168